David Viner is a museums & heritage consultant, freelance curator and writer from his home in Cirencester. He has enjoyed a career in local government museums over thirty-five years, mostly in the Cotswolds but starting off (however briefly) in Dorset where his interest in the county's roads and tracks was first encouraged. People with knowledge and experience proved very willing to share, not least Professor Ronald Good whose magisterial *The Old Roads of Dorset* provided both challenge and inspiration. Christopher Taylor's *Dorset* in the Making of the English Landscape series (first published in 1970 and recently reprinted in paperback by The Dovecote Press) proved equally inspirational. Whenever possible since then, visits to Dorset have included studies of the old routes, and this small volume is in appreciation of that support freely given. David Viner is a Fellow of the Museums Association and the Society of Antiquaries and the author of a dozen books and photographic albums. He is Chairman of the Milestone Society, campaigning for the recording, conservation and enjoyment of roadside heritage across the United Kingdom, and jointly edits the Society's journal, *Milestones and Waymarkers*.

Following page
Ackling Dyke, one of the most spectacular sections of surviving Roman road, out of use as a through route since the fifth century.

ROADS, TRACKS & TURNPIKES

DAVID VINER

THE DOVECOTE PRESS

'A road is a living thing and gathers about itself a personality as long as it is being used. Now only a thin ghost of their one time importance lingers about the old trackways.'

H.W. Timperley and Edith Brill, *Ancient Trackways of Wessex*

'The history of roads is not the study of the dead past but of the living present.'

Christopher Taylor, *Roads & Tracks of Britain*

William Barnes' delightful line drawing of a tollhouse and turnpike gate on a Vale of Blackmoor Turnpike document.

First published in 2007 by The Dovecote Press Ltd
Stanbridge, Wimborne, Dorset BH21 4JD

ISBN 9781904349143

Typeset in Monotype Sabon
Printed and bound by Baskerville Press, Salisbury, Wiltshire

All papers used by The Dovecote Press are natural, recyclable products made from wood grown in sustainable, well-managed forests

A CIP catalogue record for this book is available from the British Library

1 3 5 7 9 8 6 4 2

CONTENTS

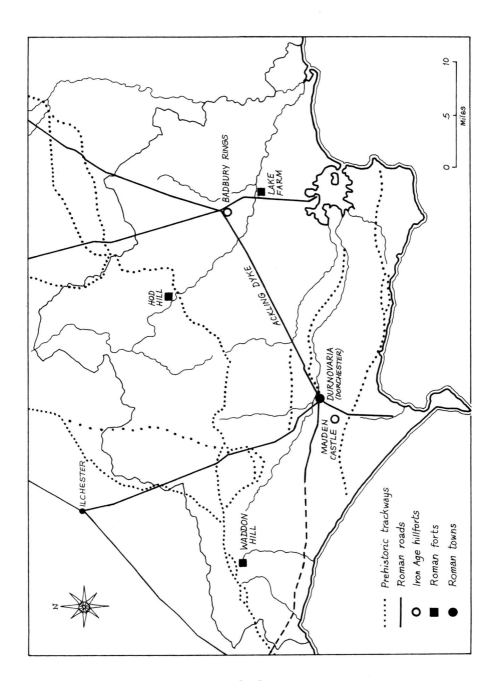

INTRODUCTION

'The turnpike-road became a lane, the lane a cart-track, the cart-track a
bridle-path, the bridle-path a footway, the footway overgrown.'
Michael Henchard visits Mr Fall the conjurer in
The Mayor of Casterbridge by Thomas Hardy (1886).

For those interested in the history of the road system, the evidence is
all around. Unlike perhaps students of canal and railway history,
where the evidence is much more spatially confined, the seeker after
old roads has the entire landscape to study and wander through, map
in hand, always aware that modern roads and routes simply continue
the practices of travellers over thousands of years.

The West Country in general, and Wessex in particular, has long
been regarded as a superb area for the research and enjoyment of
roads and tracks, both ancient and modern. The historic county of
Dorset is at its heart some 974 square miles of varied geology,
providing upland expanse, lowland vale, heathland and an impressive
coastline. Travellers crossed this landscape for an enormous variety of
reasons, as they still do today, and unravelling this continuous overlay
of evidence is part of the challenge of the road historian, and certainly
provides a great deal of enjoyment.

As Christopher Taylor rightly observed, this is a study about the
living present, not a fossilised past, despite Timperley and Brill's rather
mournful evocation of former times, which is quoted on page 4
(opposite the Contents). Roads are in themselves notoriously difficult
to date and the challenge is to unpick each in sequence, accepting that
roads and tracks do not fit easily into a simple classification of periods

Opposite page Map showing the principal Prehistoric and
Roman routes in Dorset.

of historical time and activity.

We are of course trying to cover some five thousand years or more of history. Certain prehistoric routes may still be in use today, in one way or another; many of the Roman roads across Dorset certainly are, in some instances as major highways. The vast network of lanes and tracks which we associate with the Saxon period onwards remain largely in place, but changed in small but sometimes significant ways in later periods. Not least, the turnpike routes remain the backbone of the modern system. Today we build by-passes, dual carriageways and motorways to make our travelling even quicker, although Dorset still has no designated motorways within its boundaries.

A drive along the Old Sherborne Road north from Dorchester or the similar hilltop route between Blandford and Shaftesbury are reminders of earlier routes, augmented if not replaced by the later turnpike road doing much the same journey but in the valley below. Although largely skirting Dorset proper, and one of the nearest things to a motorway in these parts, the A303 reflects its accumulated history as a through route created from a variety of earlier routes, still apparent with careful study. Across Blackmore Vale and throughout West Dorset the old ways are everywhere to be found, lanes and tracks meandering from one place to another, timelessly.

In the work of Dorset writers we also have a rich harvest. William Barnes (1800-86) and Thomas Hardy (1840-1928) in particular capture some memorable images of travelling and travellers in the county, with a fondness for the green and quiet ways, so often then passing out of use. From them they each drew inspiration. Although not born in Dorset, John Cowper Powys (1872-1963) shared that same fascination, remembering his schooldays at Sherborne. Each touches upon the special character of tracks and footpaths for country pursuits, for courting and visiting and for gatherings on high days and holidays, as well as for access to work. Often they are also seen as synonymous with the passing of the years and the cycle of life.

Respected road historians have also left their mark on Dorset, producing classic studies of their kind. The county has been very well served by the years of thorough and painstaking research published by Ronald Good and the detailed route analysis by Timperley and Brill, which in turn proved a stimulation to later studies by Cochrane and

Woodyates Inn on the Great Western Turnpike in about 1782, by Thomas Rowlandson. The inn was one of the most celebrated in Dorset, and was where George III liked to break his journey between London and Weymouth. It later became the Shaftesbury Arms, was down-at-heel when Thomas Hardy visited it in 1919, and sadly no longer stands.

particularly by Wright.

The study of roads has also attracted a fascinating 'alternative' press, where particular theories are expounded and the significance of the network of routes is interpreted as evidence of some wider human, even cosmic phenomena. The best known of these is Alfred Watkins whose book *The Old Straight Track* (1925) identified 'ley lines' across the landscape, incorporating the place name element 'ley' or 'lee' or forming a joined-up line of monuments and landscape features such as hillforts, barrows and churches. R. Hippisley Cox in his *The Green Roads of England* (1914) had been equally enthusiastic about camps, mounds and tracks, much of his evidence drawn from Wessex. Widely discredited as fanciful by other specialists, these nevertheless remain examples of the fascination for 'old roads' in the eye of the beholder.

All such studies, together with other material listed under Further Reading, provide a rich resource for the interested reader, walker and researcher to enjoy.

READING THE EVIDENCE

Maps are the place to start for road research. Opening up the latest version of any Ordnance Survey map is to disgorge a myriad of routes, colour coded with increasing variety. Together with motorway blue, we now have green for primary routes alongside the more familiar red, yellow and brown. Early mapmakers and compilers of road books first gave us the framework on which all this is based. Christopher Saxton was the first to produce a printed set of county maps, that for Dorset in 1575, followed by the maps which accompanied William Camden's masterly *Britannia,* first published with a set of county maps in 1607. However it is John Ogilby (1600-76) who is perhaps the best known. He was appointed Cartographer to King Charles II in 1666 and in the following decade his great work *Britannia* was the first detailed road survey for England and Wales and the first to use the statute mile. Ogilby and his surveyors were extremely accurate, surveying by theodolite and recording mileages on a hand-propelled measuring wheel called a dimensurator. Presented as vertical scroll maps of the main roads, the seven major cross-Dorset routes were included, such as London to Weymouth and Bristol to Weymouth. Themselves of great antiquity, they formed the backbone of the subsequent evolution of the system throughout the county.

Better roads meant more travellers, for business as well as pleasure, and the demand for maps and surveys grew. Thomas and John Osborne's map of 1748 showed a largely pre-turnpike road system, including a main route linking Evershot, Cerne Abbas and Milton Abbas with Blandford. The changes which followed are best appreciated in the work of Isaac Taylor, a road surveyor by profession. He produced various county maps, including Hampshire in 1759 and Dorset in 1765, the first map of the county on the now familiar one-inch to one-mile scale. Taylor also showed the old as well as the new routes, making his work doubly valuable.

A section from Isaac Taylor's 1765 map of Dorset, showing both old routes and new turnpikes. The Great Western Turnpike of 1753-54, which started at Salisbury and ended west of Bridport, is shown crossing the map diagonally toward the top right hand corner. The Roman road to Poole is marked on the right, east of Badbury Rings and Kingston Hall (Kingston Lacy).

The cartographer Daniel Paterson (1739-1825) produced the first of his Route Books in 1771, superseding Ogilby and reflecting the development of the turnpike system at that time. The best-known edition of his work is that of 1829 which shows the road network just at the point at which the railway system began to take its toll on roads and road usage. *Paterson's Roads* continued to be the standard work until and after the maps of the Ordnance Survey began in the nineteenth century.

Further useful information comes from the standard contemporary Dorset histories of which Hutchins *History and Antiquities of the County of Dorset* (1774) is pre-eminent. It incorporated the county map of John Bayly, well placed to catch the first fruits of turnpike development in the county, and to include such features in his maps. Like Paterson, John Cary was influential; he was contracted to undertake a survey of all the main roads in the country, resulting in his *New Map* of 1794, a detailed and accurate work much reprinted.

There are also the travellers, who left behind written evidence of their experiences and descriptions of the state of the roads, particularly in the sixteenth to eighteenth centuries. For the turnpike era and later road development, there is a mass of surviving primary literature and records. Parliamentary papers, turnpike acts, the minutes and accounts of individual turnpike trusts and the whole range of county council records from the later nineteenth century onwards all provide information. Consulted in record office or local library archive, these make fascinating reading, putting flesh on the bare bones of the road network.

With all this to hand, nothing is better than a physical examination of the landscape itself, as time, access and mobility allow. Dorset is very well served by rights of way, as any examination of a modern map will show, and many of these follow old footpaths and tracks. Their variety across the county also reflects the geological variations influencing the landscape, so that a walk deep in the vale or up on the breezy chalklands can still evoke a sense of place and of history. A number of such walks are suggested later on in this book.

Finally, a note on measured distances, which varied throughout history. The Roman mile was based upon the 1,000 paces of a runner's stride at five feet. Thus it was slightly shorter, at some 1,620 English yards, than the 1,760 yards of the statute mile which was first defined by statute in 1593 and adopted nationally in 1824, one aim being to stop 'great confusion and manifest frauds'. Prior to that, numerous local variations persisted around the United Kingdom, such as the old English or customary mile of some 2,428 yards. From the mid seventeenth century, the developing postal system, the spread of the turnpikes and the appearance of increasingly sophisticated maps all encouraged standardisation, which continues in use where the imperial system survives today. Metrication however threatens to remove its evidence as a new European-wide influence is brought to bear.

PREHISTORIC TRACKS

To most people, prehistoric routes suggest upland un-metalled ways, crossing the landscape in bold sweeps, undeterred by physical barriers. The modern designation of a number of these as parts of long-distance walking routes only adds to this concept, for example the Great Ridgeway being styled the Wessex Ridgeway on maps and signposts. This is a good thing, presenting opportunities for access which have not always been available.

This particular route can be followed on foot and along minor roads right across Dorset from the north east of the county near Shaftesbury to the Devon border west of Lyme Regis. Often called the oldest road in Britain, it runs from beyond the Chilterns across the Thames Valley and along the Berkshire Ridgeway (another easily

The Ridgeway near Ringmoor, looking north east towards Okeford Fitzpaine, with Hambledon Hill in the distance. Was this once also a Roman route from Hod Hill to Rawlsbury hillfort?

accessible section) into Wessex.

H.W. Timperley walked the downs across Dorset and especially Wiltshire for years before his study with Edith Brill was published some forty years ago. Their great work *Ancient Trackways of Wessex* gives a really detailed account of the routes. Timperley could see the effect of ploughing up the old downland and sheepwalks during both the First and the Second World Wars, eroding many an old green road; his work is a reminder that what survives today is a relic of a former and busier landscape.

What were these routes for originally? We are trying to cover here several thousand years of prehistory, from the Neolithic through to the early years of the Roman invasion. The received wisdom about trackways across the Wessex downs is that ridgeway routes suggest long distance links, using the open uplands for communication and the movement of animals, keeping clear of more inaccessible valley bottoms, where conditions were much harder and tree and scrub cover more impenetrable.

The surviving ancient monuments provide the best evidence we have and act as focal points, to which we can add the ever-increasing amount of knowledge from archaeological excavation of settlement sites – both on the downs and in the valleys. Burial mounds from the neolithic and the bronze age are intimately related to the Dorset ridgeway landscape, icons on the skyline and clues to a more complicated story than we have yet unravelled.

Farming patterns evolved and land was taken into cultivation; access was required and trade encouraged – all factors which stimulate the development of tracks linking communities in a more permanent fashion. As settlement patterns continued to evolve, so too did a system of routes providing the links. The trackways which earlier writers have so admired are just part – albeit a spectacular part – of this larger picture.

Names are given to particular routes, so as well as the Great Ridgeway we have the Coastal Ridgeway (in more modern styling the South Dorset Ridgeway), and the Salisbury Way, a thirteen-mile ridge route with prehistoric origins and later an Anglo-Saxon boundary. Such names may or may not confer a sense of antiquity and often come into use later than the route itself, but they do create a sense of

Common Water Lane. The old Ridgeway looking east from Broadwindsor up onto Horn Hill.

linear continuity across the landscape. This too might well be misleading. It suggests, for example, that these routes are contemporary or have a relationship to each other, which they may well not have, at least not over any length of time. We can only suppose that the Great Ridgeway was a through route; it cannot be proved.

Perhaps the most spectacular of all is the Coastal Ridgeway across the southern downlands of the county. This extends from the coast at Ballard Down above Swanage via the Corfe Castle gap and across Purbeck and the dramatic coastline west of Lulworth. Running above Weymouth Bay, it extends to the west in equally spectacular fashion over Black Down to reach the coast again above Abbotsbury. As an experience in tracing high level, long-distance prehistoric routes, it can hardly be bettered.

The Harrow Way (or Hard Way) is a variant off the Ridgeway, an east-west route through Hampshire and Wiltshire taking a south-westerly route across Dorset through Halstock and Corscombe to join the Ridgeway up on Toller Down.

Other names on the map are clues to later significant use of a particular cross-country route. The Ox-Drove is more readily associated with the drove roads of later medieval and early modern times, moving cattle and sheep to market. It no doubt follows a well-established route, joining with the Ridgeway and a later Roman road at Win Green, a hill-top junction of ways above Ashmore. Such joining of ways can indeed be evocative of past activity.

There are many other examples, some now masked by modern impositions such as by-passes and other landscape changes. The Puddletown ridgeway follows an east-west route over the downs, as a green lane and a footpath. Its route can be traced across three river valleys to gain the higher ground north west of Maiden Newton. Later used in part as a coach road, its real significance is as an earlier long-distance route. Another heathland example is the ridgeway route between the Frome and Piddle valleys from Wareham across to Tincleton and thence to Dorchester and beyond.

ROMAN ROADS

Straight lines on any road map are invariably defined as of Roman origin. Often this is true, but we should beware of the equally well-delineated enclosure roads of the eighteenth and nineteenth centuries and many of the turnpike routes, similarly engineered.

The Roman network was based upon the needs of military conquest and the advance of the Roman army across the south west of England in the invasion period from 43 AD onwards. As such its construction was largely the work of army surveyors and engineers. No less than with prehistoric routes, interpretations differ as new evidence comes to light, but the most significant features seem clear.

The main Roman highway was the east-west route from Old Sarum (the prehistoric and Roman fortified site of *Sorviodunum* north of Salisbury) to another equally significant and impressive hillfort at Badbury Rings, north west of Wimborne. Air photographs show a confluence of routes here, adjoining the hillfort defences.

Several routes can be identified. The destination of at least one in this early conquest period appears to have been Poole Harbour where a port (and perhaps a military landing base) had long been suggested at Hamworthy. In addition, excavations have revealed a substantial conquest fort at Lake near Wimborne, occupied by the Second Augustan Legion, which was intimately involved in the conquest of the south west. So this may have been the real focal point.

Another route on a north-south alignment comes down from the Bath and Bristol region towards Poole Harbour via Badbury, and has been associated with the need to extract and transport the rich resources of lead from the Mendips. Such mineral wealth provided one of the attractions to the Roman imperial authorities for a conquest of Britain.

A third and equally important route marks the advance westwards via what became the regional capital at Dorchester, and was principally aimed at Exeter, the fortress home of the Second Legion for a significant part of this conquest period in the 50s and 60s AD. Once completed, this road across the county became the principal link between the West Country and the centre of provincial administration based in London.

Much of this Roman network so far described has long been out of use, and thus provides a rare opportunity to examine sections of well-preserved Roman roads not masked by modern needs. Only a small section of the Old Sarum-Badbury route is followed by the A354, near Woodyates. Going south-westwards from Oakley Down, it is possible to trace and for some nine miles to walk along Ackling Dyke, 'one of the most magnificent stretches of undamaged Roman road in Britain' as Dorset archaeologist Bill Putnam describes it. Unused since the fifth century, this massive linear bank is over 40 ft across and in places stands up to 5 ft in height (*for illustration see page 2*).

This section also reveals the engineering skills which were used to make and maintain these major routes. Foundations were laid and a hard stone or chalk surface created, sometimes with a light gravel topping. Elsewhere a metalled surface of stones or flints would be used, such material quarried from close by. Side ditches created a drainage system. The resulting causeway shows as an agger, or raised bank, particularly clear along parts of Ackling Dyke where it has not been so badly eroded as elsewhere. Despite the width of the causeway, the road itself may have been little more than ten feet wide, narrow to modern eyes.

As Ackling Dyke, the Dorchester road continues west from Badbury and can also be traced as a virtually straight line for nineteen miles across the map, although other than the first section into Shapwick very little is accessible. In Puddletown Forest, there is a noticeable zig-zag in the line, a good example of a change in alignment to accommodate a steep slope or valley crossing. Direct routes did not necessarily always mean straight lines.

Sections of Roman road have been excavated at various places in Dorset. The earlier road surfaces do not always survive, when cut into by later improvements, but in Thorncombe Wood near Thomas Hardy's birthplace at Higher Bockhampton, a well-preserved section was examined, complete with wheel ruts in the gravel surface. In fact Hardy has a splendid reference to a section of

Roman roads meet at Badbury Rings. Ackling Dyke runs from bottom left to top right and just encroaches upon the hillfort defences. In the foreground it crosses the road from the fortress at Lake towards Bath.

Roman road, perhaps this one, in his poem 'The Roman Road' in *Time's Laughingstocks* [1909]: 'The Roman Road runs straight and bare / As the pale parting-line in hair / Across the heath'.

Dorchester or *Durnovaria* was developed as the capital or regional tribal centre and so became a focus of routes and a substantial walled town. In plan we can see how the layout evolved, the street system and the positions of the gates, from which led out the main routes from the east, to the west and the north-west and to the south.

Heading for Exeter, the old line of the A35 follows the Roman as a direct route west from Dorchester, and despite modern developments at Poundbury offers a good visible alignment as far as Lamberts Hill, where an even more interesting section makes for higher ground and becomes the route to Eggardon hillfort as far as Two Gates. This probably mirrors a prehistoric ridgeway route (it certainly is a parish boundary in later centuries) but as the ridge of chalk downland gives way to the broken country of small hills and vale in West Dorset the line of this road remains unclear. Its original engineering must have been a considerable challenge across this landscape.

The other principal Roman routes in the county are south from Dorchester to what must have been a harbour base in Weymouth Bay, a route still in use today, and north west to the smaller Roman town at Ilchester or *Lindinis*, a line mirrored by the present A37. This latter route left via the west gate and within three miles had to cross the line of the town's aqueduct no less than five times. Modern maps still mark the older name of Long Ash Lane for a section of this road where it forms the western boundary of Sydling St Nicholas parish. Hardy was familiar with this name too, capturing in his writings the changing fortunes of this road since its Roman days. *Tess of the d'Urbervilles* crossed this 'straight and deserted Roman road' on her journey from Blackmore Vale to Emminster (Beaminster).

Although largely outside the county, the Fosse Way was a very significant Roman route, a 208-mile cross-country line from Lincoln and thence the Humber down to the coast in the valley of the Axe. Its remarkably direct alignment can be followed today along a section of the A303 near Ilchester. Unlike so many other Roman roads, radiating from the south east, this one does not and its history has been much argued over. It seems to have been part of the barrier zone of the early Roman frontier (but not perhaps the frontier itself) created at a critical point in the conquest of Britain in the mid first century AD. If this is so, the triumphant suppression and inclusion of the local tribe in the Dorset area, the Durotriges, was sufficiently achieved by this date for the Fosse Way to include this whole area within its controlled zone.

Other than the roads themselves, very little other material evidence survives, although the county can boast two possible Roman milestones (or perhaps they were boundary markers?), from over a hundred known from Roman Britain. A fragment was found during excavations in Dorchester, and was inscribed 'dedicated to the emperor Postumus Augustus', dating it to c.260-269 AD. This probably refers to repairs to the road rather than original construction. It is not known where it might have stood originally, but it may be linked to a renewal of quarrying activity in Purbeck by the Roman authorities.

The other stone is better known and can still be seen, resited just on

The Roman milestone on the Dorchester side of the Stinsford roundabout.

the Dorchester side of the Stinsford roundabout on the by-pass (SY 708913), on the line of the Roman road into *Durnovaria*. Cylindrical but lacking any inscription, the Roman origins of this 5ft 10ins stone column are not conclusively established although it seems a good candidate. Its original siting might well have been one Roman mile from the town. Unlike later milestones from the turnpike system, Roman stones did not primarily record distances but were erected as symbols of loyalty to the emperor of the day, either inscribed or perhaps painted. As emperors changed, so too did the inscription.

This organised and systematically developed road network is nevertheless still only part of the whole story. For example, there would have been a network of local roads giving access to the industrial areas on Purbeck where stone was extracted and carted away for use elsewhere. Access to sea routes from small harbours along the Dorset coast should also be included as part of this transport network.

Certainly the principal Roman routes were overlain upon a detailed mass of prehistoric tracks, which continued to be used and which it can be argued remain in use today as the basis of our county road system. The total network for the Roman period can probably never be completely identified on a map, although the clues all lie within the modern detailed Ordnance Survey mapping system, for which the first edition of the one-inch map was published for Dorset in 1811.

MEDIEVAL ROUTES

We must remember that, with the exception of well-engineered Roman roads, most tracks and other routes remained without a proper surface right up until the eighteenth century and often beyond. Complaints about the difficulties of travel and especially poor maintenance are commonplace throughout recorded British history, and provide one of the principal sources of evidence.

The organisation which lay behind the maintenance of the Roman road network had gone (at least in recognisable form) by the fifth century AD, and for the following one thousand years or more the picture is one of an existing network continuing in use, being expanded as required, but certainly not subject to any nationwide imposition of standards.

Some sections, at least of the Roman system, clearly did go out of use. The construction of the defensive Bokerly Dyke, for example, blocked the main Roman road in the north east of the county in the early post-Roman period (at SU 033198) effectively isolating the long section of Roman road preserved today. As settlements and markets changed, other routes simply fell out of use, un-maintained during periods of turmoil and becoming irrelevant thereafter.

Saxon place names can help the identification of routes. They are also reminders of the changing pattern of settlement in the countryside, of the emergence of villages and the growth of towns. Roads and tracks served such communities, essentially for local administrative and market needs. They also linked individual farmsteads, in meandering fashion as settlement expanded into forest and waste woodland. They may even have originated as double-ditched boundaries between farms. Marshwood Vale has plenty of examples worth exploring, such as the several lanes between Whitchurch Canonicorum and Stoke Abbott.

Here-paeth or Herepath is a fairly common road name in Saxon land charters, which survive from the eighth century onwards. It indicates a route of primarily military purpose or a through route, later in common use. Reference is often made to 'wegs' or ways along territory boundaries, which may indicate access routes. The use of the word *straet* may suggest a deliberately constructed road as opposed to a track and is also used to refer to existing Roman roads, hence such names as Stratton north west of Dorchester.

We might imagine that much of our present day road system was complete by the eleventh century. Certainly, an increasing amount of documentary evidence adds to our knowledge from the Norman Conquest onwards. This supports the emergence of towns such as Shaftesbury, Wareham, Wimborne and Bridport as the backbone of the network, often with military importance. Defended sites such as Corfe Castle were also developed as towns, some more planned than others. Shaftesbury may have had a population of over a thousand at the time of Domesday in 1086.

Another hugely significant factor was the influence of the monasteries, which were not only centres of learning but economic focal points and centres of considerable trading activity. Enormous influence could be exerted by the communication needs between parent abbeys and their scattered estates and properties. Many were large-scale farming operations, with extensive interests in sheep and wool production. Glastonbury Abbey had estates at Buckland Newton and Sturminster Newton, concentrating largely on sheep.

The Cistercian Order carefully selected remote situations for abbeys at Bindon and Forde, and a house for nuns at Tarrant Crawford, each carrying with it a need to ensure and maintain a proper route network as well. All this was doubtless based upon existing routes, many of them cross-country. As an example of scale, around 1330 the flocks on the Bindon Abbey estates totalled some 7,000 sheep.

Cerne Abbas, in its own river valley, had long been a focus for a number of routes, not only the north-south route along the valley floor (the present A352) but a number of cross-routes coming over from the neighbouring valleys on either side and beyond. Like other Dorset Benedictine houses, Cerne Abbey was refounded on a grand scale in the tenth century, opening up the richest period for this community. After the Dissolution of the Monasteries (here in 1539) Cerne faded

White Mill Bridge at Sturminster Marshall, a late 12th century bridge across the River Stour.

from its earlier significance. Nor did Cerne benefit from the coming of the railways in the nineteenth century, and so presents a fascinating study of former greatness. Its road system, however, continues very much in use.

A glance at the map shows this pattern even more clearly in the neighbouring Piddle valley where cross routes abound, as well as routes following the river valley, and servicing not merely the valley communities such as Piddletrenthide and Alton Pancras but the wider network too. Some routes between monastic houses have a distinctly cross-country feel about them, such as that between Abbotsbury and Cerne.

The chalk hills and valleys of mid Dorset sustained a patchwork of local routes between communities, many of which suffered substantial change through the medieval period. This reflected changes in settlement pattern, land ownership and the decline and shift in population. Shrunken or 'lost' villages can still be traced in the low earthworks and surviving old place names, in the Milborne and Upper Winterborne valleys especially. The road network of today, with its rights of way codes and issues of public and private ownership, is but a shadow of what once was a much more complicated web of tracks and footpaths used by the community at large.

Of the permanent structures, bridges are by far the most significant and longlasting; they were essential aids to travel. Dorset has some

The packhorse bridge over the River Tarrant at Tarrant Monkton.

fine medieval examples, especially White Mill Bridge at Sturminster Marshall which dates from 1175 and is graceful as well as functional. Upstream, nearby Crawford Bridge at Spetisbury, also over the River Stour, is some sixty years later in date, although each has of course been periodically rebuilt over the years. Such repairs are not just a modern activity; one Richard Bryan left three shillings in his will in 1341 for the repair of White Mill Bridge, a substantial structure 12 ft wide between its parapets and broad for a medieval bridge.

Other bridges served lesser routes such as packhorse ways, and there are good examples at Fifehead Neville, only 6 ft wide, and Tarrant Monkton, even less. The cost of bridge construction was borne from various sources, by local landowners as well as by the monasteries and churches. Tolls could also be charged and there is a longstanding tradition of paying for bridge maintenance in this way, which still continues around the country today.

Bridges are also indicators of older routes, surviving because to replace them would be costly. Although relatively minor in importance today, the routes over the Stour at White Mill and Crawford Bridges link directly not only with the earlier network of routes to and around Badbury Rings but more significantly perhaps to Wimborne and to Cranborne, growing in importance as focal points. In turn the growth of nearby Blandford as a market town from the thirteenth century took away some of the traffic, allowing these two bridges to survive unchanged albeit less significant for so long.

Attempts were made to allocate responsibilities for road upkeep. The Statute of Winchester of 1285 made manorial landowners responsible, which included monasteries and churches. It also attempted to ensure that the threat from highwaymen and robbers was reduced, by decreeing a minimum width of 200 ft to be kept clear on each side of the road. The Statute made another stipulation, that if a track or bridleway became blocked a new route should be made alongside the original – thus new routes, encouraged by statute and custom, evolved as rights of way, meandering around obstacles and blockages.

Across Dorset the state of the roads varied according to the local geology and terrain. In the clay lands of the vales of Blackmore and further west in Marshwood, deep winding lanes are the key feature. Their age is almost impossible to tie down, but centuries of continuous use and erosion leave many as holloways, deeply embedded into the landscape. Steep banks, frequently tree covered, indicate just how much erosion has occurred, through use and weathering. West Dorset has many fine examples. Norway Lane, a corruption of North Way Lane, climbs the bank for over a mile out of Stoke Abbott up to Stoke Knap, providing the link with nearby Broadwindsor, and is a classic of its type. Erosion continues still.

The growth of medieval towns as market centres had considerable influence on communications. New boroughs with market status were established in a dozen places, not all of them successfully. Whilst Blandford, Lyme Regis, Poole, Sherborne and Weymouth are all recognisable today, others such as Charmouth, Corfe Castle and Whitchurch Canonicorum remained as villages.

The medieval market significance of Beaminster, Bere Regis, Cranborne and Evershot is also less obvious today, except for clues in the street layout. Beaminster's market place and the open central areas in Maiden Newton and Cranborne provide the evidence, the latter especially important as the centre for the extensive royal hunting grounds of Cranborne Chase. In 1542 the traveller John Leland notably described Evershot as a 'very unpretentious and poor market town'.

Some places had especial significance as pilgrimage routes. The

Deep lanes like Norway Lane, a holloway linking Stoke Abbott with Broadwindsor, are the result of erosion and centuries of use.

shrine of St. Candida made Whitchurch Canonicorum a focal point for travellers to the thirteenth century shrine. Shaftesbury was another religious centre, attracting pilgrims to the sanctuary of Edward the Martyr, murdered at Corfe in 978.

Fairs were an important feature of medieval life, attracting large numbers of people to a given spot each year. Perhaps the best known is Woodbury Fair, its market charter dating back to 1232 and held over five days every year amongst the ancient earthworks on Woodbury Hill outside Bere Regis. Thomas Hardy walked the thirteen miles from Dorchester to the fair in 1873, when thousands of sheep were still being sold, with stalls and a fair to refresh and entertain.

The expression 'The King's Highway' is a reminder of the influence

Broke Lane at West Hall Farm, near where it turns into Green Lane. This now little-used lane was once the main medieval road between Dorchester and Sherborne.

of the monarch on the road network, defining a perpetual right of passage for the sovereign and his subjects over another person's landholding. Royal Itineraries around the country also affected Dorset, King John favouring the hunting grounds on Cranborne Chase and in the thirteenth century Edward I was a frequent visitor to the religious houses at Bindon and Tarrant Crawford.

The historically important Gough's Map of about 1360 shows some 3,000 miles of English roads. Five main routes are shown out of London, including the road to Exeter and into Cornwall by way of Winchester, Salisbury, Shaftesbury, Sherborne, Crewkerne and Honiton. This is the Exeter Road, an immensely important route in the opening up the whole of the West Country during and beyond the medieval period, and later used as a coach and post route. A particular feature was the Sherborne Causeway, much altered but once a raised paved road over some twelve miles, constructed (or reconstructed?) under an act of 1554.

Most of the medieval roads between the principal medieval towns are still in use today. Some have changed, notably the route between

West Street, Corfe Castle in 1890. Until the 18th century this was Corfe's principal thoroughfare, and was once busy with waggons laden with stone from Purbeck's quarries.

Dorchester and Sherborne which followed the higher ground of a probable prehistoric ridge route as the Old Bath Road (later Old Sherborne Road) as far as Middlemarsh. From here to Sherborne its line has been obscured by later land enclosures, but the route can be traced by minor roads and paths into Sherborne, for example along Broke Lane and Green Lane. The turnpike upgrading and part-replacement of 1752-3 ran further to the west and created a largely new line for the whole route, itself re-aligned in 1848.

The timelessness of routes across the landscape is nowhere better seen than on the Isle of Purbeck, where land boundaries and access ways are often synonymous. Corfe Castle was the natural focus of routes because of its siting at the gap in the chalk ridge. Tied into the significant coastal traffic it generated, the requirements of the quarrying trade engaged in extracting the much esteemed Purbeck stone, or 'marble', included west-east as much as north-south links over the stone plateau between the various communities. Marblers' routes also criss-crossed Corfe Common to and from the small town.

The Priests Way, as it is now styled, is one such – so named because

The Priests Way across Purbeck near Blacklands. Throughout the middle ages this was the track used by the priest at Worth Matravers to serve the small chapel at Swanage.

until 1506 it was used by the priest at Worth Matravers to serve the small chapel at Swanage, then a much smaller place than it later became. This splendidly emphasises the dominance of stone in this landscape, limestone walls to either side. Also on Purbeck is one of Dorset's finest examples of a causeway, built up to create a road across marshy ground. From South Bridge in Wareham, the causeway extends some 800 ft to Stoborough village across the River Frome flood plain.

In the sixteenth century significant legislation was introduced to try to improve the upkeep of roads. A statute of 1555 described highways as 'being now very noisome and tedious to travel in and dangerous to all passengers and carriages'. It codified existing practice by requiring parishes to be made liable for the upkeep of highway routes passing through their area of responsibility (the byways being left in the care of landowners). Individual parishioners holding land of an annual value of £50 or more were to be obliged to provide four consecutive days each year working on the roads and providing their own equipment. Eight years later this system of Statute Labour was increased to six days each year. A Surveyor of Highways or Waywarden was to be appointed to oversee the work and to make three inspections each year. No specification of standards was provided and the task was unpaid, a recipe for procrastination and avoidance which exposed an inherent weakness in the system.

Individuals commuted their responsibility for cash to pay others to undertake the work; able-bodied paupers of the parish were often used as a labour force, paid very little for their efforts. Left to their own devices, local communities would tend to concentrate their energies for the greatest benefit to themselves, so that should a main highway pass through a parish but not directly through the village it might remain neglected to the disadvantage of long-distance travellers passing by. One example is the nine miles or so high-level Crewkerne road beyond Maiden Newton, avoiding villages.

Most travellers made their way on horseback, with goods transported by lines of heavily laden packhorses. The increasing use from the sixteenth century onwards of four-wheeled road waggons, heavy and lumbering, added to the deteriorating conditions. No small number of horses were required to haul them – six, eight or ten were common. The effect upon the road surfaces can be imagined, especially in wet weather.

One response to such debilitating effects was to try to regulate the number of animals – horses or oxen – used as beasts of burden and so reduce the damage to road surfaces. In 1618 a limit of five horses was imposed on four-wheeled wagons. Such restrictions on the number to be used, on the weights of loads to be carried and by requiring an increase in the wheel widths of vehicles were all examples of this constraining approach, each in its own way avoiding the key issue, that of adapting the construction of the road surface to suit the developing traffic. The several later eighteenth century Broad Wheel Acts, consolidated in 1767, were classic examples of this, directed against the narrow wheel for the damage it could cause and encouraging both very broad wheels of nine inches and large horse teams.

TRAVELLING AND TRAVELLERS

The written experiences of travellers on the medieval and post-medieval road system are particularly useful and illuminating. They certainly indicate the poor state of much of the road system despite the legislative attempts to make improvements.

John Leland (1506?-52) is especially interesting. He became Antiquary to King Henry VIII with the authority to search the records held in cathedrals and monasteries, and travelled around the country on horseback in the period 1533-43. His *Itinerary* became Britain's first road book. Leland's best recorded Dorset travels took place in 1542. An outward circuit in the north of the county led to a good description of Sherborne, including the causeway and a reference to Five Bridges on the Shaftesbury road. On his return journey he crossed Dorset from Lyme to Poole, Wimborne and Cranborne.

Leland's route stuck to the coastal ways from Lyme to Bridport, thence inland in a large loop to Beaminster, across to Evershot and back down (avoiding Dorchester) to Weymouth and Portland. After another coastal stretch to Lulworth, he made for Wareham. Here he mentioned the difficulties of the low and marshy way towards Poole, offset by the existence of a ferry across the inlet of Lytchett Bay as a short cut.

We can also learn from later writers such as Celia Fiennes (1662-1741). Brought up on the Wiltshire/Hampshire border, she travelled throughout the country on horseback; her memoirs record journeys in Wessex from about 1685 to 1702. Travelling west from Dorchester, for example, we find that 'the ways are stony and very narrow', whilst the route to Bridport and Lyme Regis has 'very steep hills up and down'.

Daniel Defoe (1660-1731) travelled similarly around the country; his *Tour* dates from 1724-6 but reflects his earlier travels, much of it before the emergence of the turnpike system. He is critical of the poor state of the roads, noting the effects upon 'the great number of horses

The state of the roads on Portland, according to the 18th century artist Hieronymous Grimm. The view shows St George's Church, and on the left cow pats being dried out for fuel.

every year kill'd by the excess of labour in those heavy ways'. His journeys took him through Poole, Wareham ('a neat town') and westwards from Dorchester, which he also found pleasant and agreeable. Whilst in the north-west of the county, Defoe wondered how the 'long steep hill' into Yeovil called Babylon Hill got its name. Locals were unable to enlighten him.

William Stukeley (1687-1765) was a noted antiquary and another traveller on horseback, his tour mostly made in 1723. An early field archaeologist, he had an eye for Roman and early roads, spotting at Bokerly Dyke the inter-relationship between earthworks of various dates. Almost half a century later, the agricultural writer Arthur Young (1741-1820) toured in Britain and indeed Europe from 1767, and in using a light chaise for transport was well placed to compare the state of the roads before and after the turnpikes were made. He gave praise as well as criticism.

Another traveller with a good West Country interest was William Cobbett (1763-1835), a Hampshire farmer's son and a prolific campaigning writer, who largely avoided the turnpikes because he hated paying the tolls. He said 'my object was, not to see inns and turnpike-roads, but to see the country' and so he preferred going 'through the villages' as he termed the older toll-free routes. His *Rural Rides* was published in 1830, evidence of a great deal of travelling.

Equally forthright was John Byng, later Lord Torrington, who rode from London to Weymouth in 1782. He found service for an

The old coach road from Chilfrome descends to Lower Kingcombe, between the walls on the left. The present road to Maiden Newton passes to the right in front of the house, in this delightful 1938 view by Ronald Good.

individual traveller without servants difficult to obtain. Of Woodyates Inn (*see illustration on page 9*), he wrote: 'I look upon an inn as the seat of all roguery, profaness and debauchery; and sicken of them every day, by hearing nothing but oaths and abuse of each other, and brutality to horses'.

Most of these writers would have observed some effects of the changes in the landscape caused by the enclosure of open land, authorised by private agreements in the later sixteenth and seventeenth centuries and later by Acts of Parliament, in the period 1750-1850. Thus was created the field patterns which we still recognise today, incorporating but also amending the existing road and track network. The physical alignment of many straight roads, for example across the heathland, relate as much to enclosure as to later turnpike improvement.

Another good clue is a sharp right-angled bend around a field boundary or straight sections of road with wide verges. Some of these are reminders of the old drove road system, much reduced by enclosure of the open downland. Although wide verges provided grazing, the former freedom of movement for large numbers of animals to and from market thus became constrained by the combined impact of enclosure and turnpike improvement, creating a more controlled system in which the charging of tolls became achievable.

THE TURNPIKE AGE

As the first major and comprehensive improvement since the Romans, the turnpike system revolutionised the road network in Dorset as the eighteenth century progressed, as indeed it did all over the country. Traffic was increasing in line with users' requirements for both volume and speed, and that created a need for greater investment and a degree of forward planning which the old parish-based system could not offer.

This vacuum was filled by turnpike trusts, consisting of groups of trustees armed with a specific Act of Parliament to improve a specified route or routes, who borrowed or loaned money and made capital investment to improve the network. Trustees were usually local people with a direct interest in a particular road or region; often they were local landowners or gentry, whose interests might extend to local businesses in the locality which would benefit from improved road transport. Some were also county JPs, well aware of the weaknesses of the old order and supportive of an alternative method of administration.

Toll gates previously used on the road between Wimborne and Kingston Lacy, purchased by Mr Bankes' agent when the tolls were 'freed' and set up at the Home Farm on the estate.

Investment was recouped by the charging of tolls levied on traffic, according to a scale of fees which sought to cover most users, human and animal. Turnpike Acts usually lasted for twenty-one years before renewal or expiry, and provide a fascinating if complicated source of information as to how the network changed and improved, as new sections of road were added and redundant or uneconomical ones were abandoned. One of the most interesting facets is the essentially local nature of the operation, rarely consolidating into bigger units and largely retaining a distinctive character, which survives in small measure even today in what remains as evidence on the ground.

Like the canals at much the same time and the railways later on, there was a period of development mania during which a great number of acts were submitted to and approved by parliament. The busiest period for such activity in Dorset was 1750-80, the earliest act 1752/3 and the last one 1857, in all creating a total of twenty-five separate trusts with routes primarily if not completely within Dorset. Five of these, including the Chard, Yeovil and Wincanton trusts, linked or encroached from adjoining counties. All Dorset trusts had ceased to operate by the end of 1882. At its height there were about 500 miles of turnpiked road in Dorset, still only a small proportion of its total road mileage.

Much was achieved via turnpike investment in a little over a century. With finance available, surveyors were appointed and new sections of road were built as part of this improved system, although it would be a mistake to assume that all turnpiked roads were new. Improvements previously made tended to be hidden or abandoned, as can still be seen climbing West Hill in Sherborne.

Unsurprisingly, the first Dorset trust to be established was the *Shaftesbury & Sherborne Trust* (1752-3), a recognition of this long-established important through route across the north of the county, described in the act as the Great Western Post Road, reflecting its role as the Salisbury to Exeter mail route. This remains today as the A30 and was turnpiked throughout, and incorporated four side roads. This was often done to cover all aspects of likely traffic movement on and off the turnpike, in this case routes around Sherborne to

Opposite page Map showing the routes of Dorset's Turnpike Trusts.

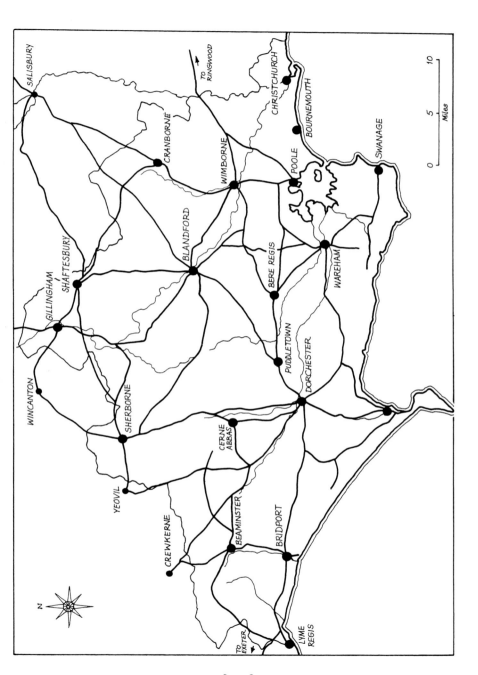

SALISBURY

TO RINGWOOD

CHRISTCHURCH

BOURNEMOUTH

CRANBORNE

WIMBORNE

POOLE

SWANAGE

Miles

0 5 10

BLANDFORD

BERE REGIS

WAREHAM

SHAFTESBURY

GILLINGHAM

PUDDLETOWN

DORCHESTER

WINCANTON

SHERBORNE

CERNE ABBAS

YEOVIL

CREWKERNE

BEAMINSTER

BRIDPORT

LYME REGIS

TO EXETER

N

Wincanton, to Longburton and to Revels Inn in Buckland Newton parish, a significant spot in Dorset turnpike history where the older great road from Dorchester to Sherborne came down into the vale. Usually the end of these specified routes was co-terminus with the same for another turnpike trust, as at Revels Inn. In 1778/9 the Trust was split into its two natural divisions based upon Shaftesbury and Sherborne, to improve administration.

Two other side routes around Shaftesbury covered the Wincanton road from there and also the road south to Melbury and beyond, where it could link with the high road south to Blandford. Over the subsequent 125 years the various parts of the Sherborne and Shaftesbury Trust, renewed no less than eight times during that period, made significant improvements including nine additions to the routes within the first three years, suggesting that the proposals had met with favour. By 1840 the Trust had some 90 miles of road in its care. It survived until 1877.

An example of new building was the straight stretch of road between Middlemarsh and Holnest (present A352), and with the inclusion after 1800 of the lower road from Shaftesbury to Blandford along the Iwerne valley it was also typical in joining up various local routes and adding in a new link between Fontmell Magna and Sutton Waldron (present A350). Both are still apparent today.

Such is the detail contained in these Acts and their various renewals that only the briefest chronology of each trust can be attempted here, with formation dates shown in brackets.

The *Harnham, Blandford and Dorchester Trust* (1753-4), also sometimes known as the Great Western Turnpike, covered the other great road from Salisbury through Dorset, now the A354 to Dorchester, extending originally to Long Bredy Hut on the A35 towards Bridport and Axminster. It had no branches but did include the old route to Beaminster from Bridport via Waytown and Netherbury, which are minor roads today. On its main route, the Trust made considerable sections of new road all the way to Dorchester, including taking a new line into Blandford from the east, thus cutting out the small town of Cranborne, previously served by this route as recorded by Ogilby. It had 48 miles in total and survived until 1879.

Lyme Regis Turnpike.

MARSHALSEA GATE.

day of _____ 187_

	No.	s.	d.
Horses drawing Carriage with springs			
Horses drawing Carriage without springs			
Horses drawing Carriage with Lime			
Horse, Mule, Ass, &c., not drawing........			
Drove of Oxen or Neat Cattle			
Drove of Calves, Sheep, &c			

This clears Blackdown Gate.

Turnpike tickets were once issued by the thousand, but are now rare. This one from the *Lyme Regis Trust* was issued in 1872, five years before it closed. Marshalsea and Blackdown are on the western edge of the Marshwood Vale on what is now the B3165.

The *Poole Trust* (1755-6), more completely called the *Poole, Wimborne and Cranborne Trust*, originally had five routes all focused upon Poole, a major port at this time. It gave a new impetus for Cranborne, including a section of new road (present B3081) linking it to the highway at Handley Hill. Sometimes routes proposed in the legislation were never built and this Trust has several examples, the triumph of aspiration (or competition) over reality. At its fullest extent the Trust had just 44 miles of road and was one of the last trusts to expire, in 1882, a reflection perhaps of the commercial nature of its role in the urban area of Poole.

The *Lyme Regis and Crewkerne Trust* (1757-8) began with only the road from Charmouth to Uplyme but later added that between Uplyme and Crewkerne, skirting Marshwood Vale. That too had alternatives, including a wander around the lanes through Thorncombe from Wareham Cross through to Horn Ash. A number of interesting route names survive along this line, including Blackwater and Easthay Lanes and Venn Hill. This is described by Good as 'a fine old highway' and was discharged from the Trust's care in 1800 in favour of the present B3165 via Birdsmoorgate, previously called Furzemoorgate and itself an interesting turnpike place name.

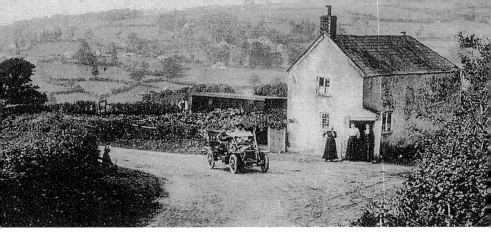

Frost's Corner old turnpike gate at the top of Colway Lane in Lyme Regis.
Here the replacement (and modern) Charmouth road opened in
the late 1920s goes off to the right, replacing the old road across
Black Ven in the foreground.

This trust had some 50 miles of road in 1854 and lasted until 1877.

One interesting aspect of its stewardship was the route around and beneath the cliffs between Charmouth and Lyme through Black Ven. As the result of landslips a new road was created in 1825 and the whole route finally abandoned in May 1924. It has now disappeared.

The *Ringwood, Longham, Leigh Trust* (1758-9) dealt with routes in the very east of the county, linking access into Dorset with the great road coming south west from Basingstoke via Winchester and Romsey. Longham linked with the Poole Trust and Leigh was on the eastern outskirts of Wimborne. Some twenty miles of route were in the county, the remainder in Hampshire, and it lasted until 1867.

The important *Weymouth, Melcombe Regis and Dorchester Trust* (1760-1) shows how the network was linking up, as this Trust covered the southern half of the Sherborne to Dorchester road (that is from Revels Inn) as well as that from Dorchester to Weymouth, thus providing the link between Weymouth and Bath and Bristol. A number of link routes around Weymouth also tidy up connections with the Great Western Turnpike, at Winterbourne Steepleton and elsewhere. Later the Osmington route to Warmwell was incorporated. The route between Weymouth and Dorchester followed the Roman line, later improved by the long hairpin and cutting over Ridgeway Hill, and northwards from the county town on the old pre-Roman hilltop line of Old Sherborne Road. It is unusual in having a surviving wayside stone with plate marking the end of the Trust, which had 34 miles in 1840 and lasted until 1878.

The *Bridport First and Second District Trusts* (1764-5) were set up by the same Act although they had almost independent existences. The First Trust's task was to take over the far west of the earlier Harnham Trust route west of Askerswell and onwards into Devon, to which was added the route between Bridport and Bridport Harbour, now West Bay. In the 1820s and 1830s considerable improvements were undertaken on what became the A35, which despite all the upgrading and by-passes since that time is still recognisably the turnpike westwards from Bridport. One of its memorable achievements was a short tunnel through Thistle Hill west of Charmouth, completed in 1832; at its opening two Exeter coaches passed each other in the tunnel.

The Second Trust also took over responsibilities, in its case the Bridport to Beaminster road, adding new routes out of the latter place including over Horn Hill to Misterton, which was also improved by the construction of a 345 ft long tunnel still in use today. The work took only ten months and was opened with some ceremony in June

The wayside stone marking the end of the *Weymouth, Melcombe Regis & Weymouth Trust* at Revels Inn.

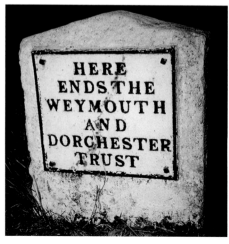

A carrier's waggon poses in front of Horn Hill tunnel
before the descent to Beaminster.

1832. Built of brick with two fine stone portals and an inscription,
the tunnel was originally lit by paraffin lamps. The previous line of
the road over the hill can still be traced.

Another significant achievement of this Trust was the creation of
an almost entirely new road via Bradpole between Bridport and
Beaminster. Today this is the A3066 and well repays study as an
example of new construction. The Trust lasted until 1881 and had 15
miles of road.

The *Blandford and Poole Trust* (1764-5) concerned itself with a
route through Corfe Mullen and Spetisbury via Bailie Gate, which
became another significant turnpike meeting place as later trusts also
came this way. This Trust's other responsibilities north and west of
Blandford later became formalised as the *Vale of Blackmoor Trust*
(1825). A proposed (but perhaps never introduced) turnpike between
Blandford and Sherborne via Hazlebury Bryan and over Bulbarrow is
a classic of its type, more optimism than sound economic sense. The
renamed trust did however create a new route from the end of the
Sherborne turnpike at Bishops Caundle via Lydlinch and Sturminster
Newton to join another existing turnpike at Durweston Bridge into

Blandford. This, plus a link northwards to Stalbridge and Henstridge (A3030 and A357) and several minor link roads authorised in the 1830s, created the pattern in use today.

Not all attempts by turnpike trusts to develop existing routes were achieved, of course. One example is the Vale of Blackmoor Trust's proposed route of 1825 via Buckland Newton and down the Piddle valley to Puddletown and Dorchester. It remained un-turnpiked and today is the B3142/3.

The *Blandford and Wimborne Trust* (1765-6) sought to develop a route on the north side of the River Stour, originally via Shapwick but actually built over ten miles via Badbury. Today this is the B3082 with its fine avenue of beech trees over two miles long west of Kingston Lacy, planted in 1835 and a strong reminder of landowner influence on the roadside.

Good described the *Wareham Trust* (1765-6) as 'one of the largest and most ambitious of Dorset turnpike trusts'. It controlled ten roads in all with up to 47 miles. Routes recognisable on the ground today include the Wareham to Swanage road, going over the hill via Kingston and only developed through Harman's Cross in post-turnpike days; and various Purbeck routes from Wareham including Stoborough to Creech, and those to East Lulworth and to Clouds Hill. The other route across the heathland, to Bere Regis, was typically carefully aligned and of simple plan and included Woodbury Hill (home of the annual fair) in its route. This last section, now by-passed, remains a good example of its type.

One of the Trust's lasting achievements was the present day north-south route (now B3075) from Spetisbury around Charborough Park and south via Sherford Bridge to Wareham. Westwards from Wareham its planned Dorchester road was incorporated only as far as Wool, its planned route via West Stafford not being further developed. The present day road via Broadmayne (A352) was the achievement of the replacement *Dorchester and Wool Trust* (1768-9). The section east of Dorchester around Whitcombe shows the greatest change from earlier routes, much of the line east of Broadmayne being upgrading of old roads. A link with West Stafford was in recognition of the former proposal, and it was this Trust which also built the link road from Warmwell to Osmington, transferred in 1782

Above left An 1872 livestock ticket issued by the Maiden Newton Trust. Hursey Gate was just west of Broadwindsor on the road to Birdsmoorgate.

Above right The plate recording the construction of the 'new road' avoiding Charminster village from 1840.

to another trust. The main line entered Dorchester at Loud's Gate, later called Max Gate.

Although its principal route remains a well-used coastal route today as the B3157, the *Abbotsbury and Bridport Trust* (1776-7) was one of the county's least successful turnpikes. Unlike most others, its original Act was not even renewed and it faded away, without even a proper name. There were the usual link routes into the main line, such as from Portesham over Black Down to reach the main west-east turnpike near Winterbourne Abbas, and a minor road up to Waddon.

Much more successful was the *Maiden Newton Trust* (1777-8) which at its most extensive had over 50 road miles and continued until the end of 1872. At its core was the main Yeovil to Dorchester road (now A37) which still contains long sections of interest. Originally it ran through Charminster village to meet the Sherborne road into Dorchester. The planned route was actually also through Maiden Newton, with the present day route coming down from Folly

[44]

Charminster toll house, built by the Maiden Newton Trust on the new
road into Dorchester avoiding the village.

Hill along what was Long Ash Lane into Grimstone being only finally
linked up in its present form in the 1930s.

The Trust also had that other splendid hill-top drive, between
Maiden Newton and Crewkerne (today's A356), giving it control of
two important routes into the county town. However it was many
years before the old coach route via Kingcombe, Hooke, Beaminster
and Mosterton faded away, perhaps an indication of the exposed
nature of the upland alternative.

Further west the Trust controlled the cross-country link between
Birdsmoorgate via Broadwindsor and thence by some new road to
Beaminster from where a further route over Beaminster Down and
round via Evershot reached Holywell, thus providing a substantial
east-west route across central Dorset. Finally there were links to
Cerne and to Frampton.

Another permanent legacy of the *Maiden Newton Trust* resulted
from its renewal act of 1840, which authorised the building of a new
road into Dorchester from just west of Charminster. This aimed to
improve access generally, cutting out the route through the village,
and not least to avoid this trust's commitment to a final mile-long
section of another trust's road into the town. Further widened and
improved since then, it remains a classic study of turnpike
development and includes a fine surviving contemporary toll house
alongside the meadows.

[45]

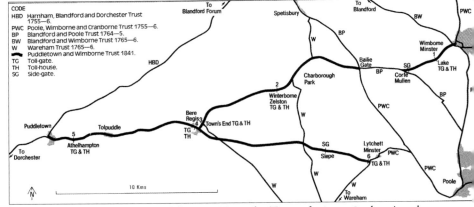

CODE
HBD Harnham, Blandford and Dorchester Trust 1755—6.
PWC Poole, Wimborne and Cranborne Trust 1755—6.
BP Blandford and Poole Trust 1764—5.
BW Blandford and Wimborne Trust 1765—6.
W Wareham Trust 1765—6.
━ Puddletown and Wimborne Trust 1841.
TG Toll-gate.
TH Toll-house.
SG Side-gate.

The Wimborne and Puddletown Turnpike Trust of 1841-78, showing the creation of new through routes.

After 1778/9 there was a pause in the expansion of Dorset's turnpike network until another flurry of activity from the 1820s. The *Cerne Abbas Trust* (1824-5) connected up various short sections over some 14 miles, which included the main valley road southwards towards Dorchester (A352). It was always therefore intimately bound up with access to and from other trust's routes. The *Bridport and Broadwindsor Trust* (1828-9) was primarily concerned with a single route (now B3162) extending into Somerset to the west of Crewkerne. This probably involved very little new road building and was essentially in competition with other existing routes.

The *Cranborne Chase and New Forest Trust* (1832) sought to improve cross-country links still further, specifically from Cann Common south east of Shaftesbury over to Tollard Royal, Sixpenny Handley and thence to Cranborne and into Hampshire. Its route identified various sections not completed (although planned) by other trusts and it controlled some 30 miles until expiry in 1877.

The *Puddletown and Wimborne Trust* (1840) was described by Good as 'the last of the ordinary Dorset trusts but one of the most important and interesting', not least because it is well documented. Created so late in the life of turnpike trusts, it had the effect of foreshadowing much of the modern road system through south central Dorset and at the same time anticipating the arrival of the

The Stag Gate at Charborough Park, built alongside
the Puddletown and Wimborne Turnpike.

railway network by only seven years. When it opened in 1847 the
Wimborne to Dorchester railway line via Wareham took away much
of the purpose of the parallel turnpike routes.

The Trust survived until 1873. Its main purpose was to create and
then monopolise the new through routes created by linking up
existing roads. Bere Regis was the hub, with new roads to Puddletown, to Lytchett Minster, and around Charborough Park to Bailie
Gate and thence to Wimborne. Some £24,000 was spent in land
acquisition and construction costs, and today this all forms part of
the A35 and the A31, a recognition of the importance of such in-
filling in the mid nineteenth century, which had the effect of turning
traffic routes through this part of the county from a north-south to a
west-east axis.

The major funder was the owner of Charborough Park, Mr J.S.W.
Sawbridge Erle Drax, who stood a considerable loss on the Trust's
overall poor finances, but who was enabled to expand his park

boundary to the north to take advantage of the alignment of the new turnpike road. He built a remarkable brick boundary wall, complete with three gates, including two commemorative arches, recording his achievement.

Dorset's final turnpike was specific to the construction of the Westham Bridge and road link in Weymouth by the *Weymouth Backwater Bridge and Road Trust* of 1857. There were of course routes within the county belonging to other trusts, particularly those in Somerset and Devon, the Axminster, Chard, Crewkerne, Yeovil and Wincanton trusts all coming into Dorset. Each can be traced as part of the road system today.

The roads themselves provide the greatest legacy of this considerable achievement, together with associated place names and any surviving roadside buildings. Place names are plentiful, such as 'The Turnpike' on Quarry Hill above Chideock on the A35, where there is still a turnpike cottage. Turnpike Cottage is not uncommon and cross roads and junctions are frequently recorded; at Dogbury Gate three roads joined, each of which had its own gate. Toller Down Gate once had a toll house at this isolated hill top crossroads.

Toll, pike or turnpike are other clues, especially at the site of a toll cottage, and Dorset still has a good surviving group of buildings despite the demands for road improvements requiring bigger and better sightlines and the removal of any impediment. Perhaps the best known by name is Max Gate, the name Thomas Hardy gave to his house on the edge of Dorchester, his home from 1885 to 1928. It was so named after one Mack, a gate keeper at the former turnpike here, which stood opposite his new home on the Wareham road. In his writings, Hardy also refers to Sherton Turnpike, the toll house still standing at West Hill, Longburton, above Sherborne, erected by the *Shaftesbury & Sherborne Trust* as part of its improvements in 1848 at the junction of the Dorchester and Blandford roads – a well known spot for many travellers.

The toll gate was central to the success of the operation, carefully sited at junctions with other routes and at the start and finish of a trust's network. The word turnpike derives from the function of the gate, turning on its 'spike' or post. Side gates or 'bars' controlled minor points of access along the route. The toll house was usually

A posed but early and informative view of a turnpike gate and toll house, at St. Margaret's in Wimborne Minster in about 1865. The Blandford road bears away to the left through the gate, and to the right towards Hillbutts and Kingston Lacy.

distinctive in shape, often with a half-hexagonal frontage to allow good sightlines each way, and with the toll board listing the charges prominently displayed. Inevitably close to the road, many toll houses were quickly cleared away once the system had come to an end, but a number do survive, including some fine eighteenth as well as nineteenth century examples.

Tolls were 'let' periodically for a fixed term, advertisements in the local paper providing a rich source of historical information. Often gates were grouped together, especially as the income stream declined, and it was not uncommon for no bidders to come forward. The process of 'farming the tolls' allowed individuals to then sub-contract the function by installing others on a short-term basis to collect money and deal with all the harassment inevitable at the toll gate. As a result, toll-keepers were often short-term tenants, their status and reputation not always in high regard.

In 1844 The *Wimborne & Puddletown Trust* found itself removing the tenants at the Lytchett gate 'in consequence of misconduct'. In fact it successfully let out its tolls for only 19 of its 37 years' existence, Mr Charles Jesty of Bere Regis performing the function of toll gatherer for much of the remainder. In recognition he became the Trust's Superintendent for the purpose as well as its surveyor.

Direction posts at significant points such as crossroads emerged in the eighteenth century, although some may well have replaced earlier examples. Defoe made an interesting observation whilst crossing the broad expanse of Salisbury Plain, without either houses or towns in view to guide him on the road, which 'often lyes very broad, and branches off insensibly, [and] might easily cause a traveller to loose his way'. This suggests a lack of signposting of some of the road junctions. Later the General Turnpike Act of 1773 required the erection of suitable informative signs for travellers.

The imposition of tolls and measurement of distances also required some form of recording along the routes and this was achieved by milestones, which varied in design and size with each turnpike trust. A General Turnpike Act of 1767 required trusts to show the names

This wood engraving by William Barnes of the short-lived prison in lower High East Street, Dorchester (built 1784 and demolished in the 1790's) also shows a nice example of a wooden finger post sign for the main Bridport-Dorchester-Blandford road.

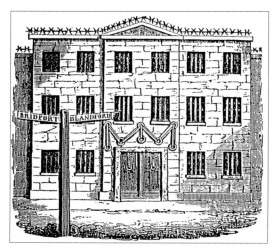

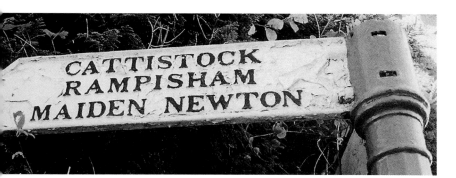

Old cast iron finger post sign in the village street at Evershot.

of main towns on their stones and runs of stones were commissioned, usually in locally sourced stone, but later also in cast iron. Relatively few of the original eighteenth century examples survive, but there is one dated 1769 in Christchurch and another just north of Shaftesbury dated 1766 on its front. Repair and renewal included repainting and re-lettering, as the *Poole Trust* is recorded as doing in 1778; 'new faced, lettered and figured' in the sum of two pounds and twelve shillings. Poole later introduced cast iron markers, also locally made, but the *Maiden Newton Trust* stuck with stone. In 1850 it had forty-three of its milestones re-lettered and painted at a cost of two pounds and three shillings.

Turnpike history perpetuated in the place name sign
at an isolated cross roads on Toller Down.

 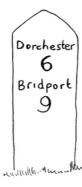 

Above left Good evidence of re-use on this six mile stone from Dorchester at Winterbourne Abbas on A35. The original face on the left has been turned round and the stone re-inscribed. Dorset has several other examples.

Above right Old style milestone near Cranborne, complete with OS bench mark

Shapes varied, the familiar tombstone pattern with inscribed Roman numerals being fairly standard. Mileages were given to relevant places in either direction and some old place names are recorded in this way, such as Shaston for Shaftesbury. Later cast iron plates were often fixed to existing stones to replace the old inscription, and sometimes the stone was turned around, hiding the old detail. There was also a general conversion of mileage distances if originally shown in Roman numerals into Arabic.

Good examples of milestones survive on the major routes especially to and from Dorchester on A35, A352 and A354, and the A35/A31 route to Wimborne and A350 Blandford to Poole. Members of the Milestone Society have been cataloguing surviving examples and campaigning for their conservation and preservation. Around 230 of the estimated original 400 survive in Dorset today.

Always historically important, the principal bridges remained under the control of the county authorities, albeit only 24 out of 438 stone bridges listed in a 1791 survey. Parishes were responsible for no less than 58% of that total. There was considerable rebuilding in the eighteenth century, all part of highway improvement. On the eastern

Grey's Bridge was built in 1748 to bring the new London Road into Dorchester directly across the water meadows rather than through Fordington, as previously.

approach into Dorchester, Grey's Bridge was newly built in 1748 to improve access into the town. Blandford Bridge was largely rebuilt over its medieval predecessor in 1783, and enlarged again in 1812. Canford Bridge at Wimborne is another good nineteenth century example.

A well known feature of Dorset bridges are the cast iron plates dating from an Act of 1828, in the name of R. Fooks, Clerk of the Peace at that time. Anyone convicted of damaging 'this county bridge' would be liable 'to be transported for life', a draconian

A number of Dorset's county bridges still have this well known 'transportation' sign of 1828; this one is on the Charminster road just outside Dorchester.

DORSET
ANY PERSON WILFULLY INJURING ANY PART OF THIS COUNTY BRIDGE WILL BE GUILTY OF FELONY AND UPON CONVICTION LIABLE TO BE TRANSPORTED FOR LIFE
BY THE COURT
7 & 8 GEO 4 C30 S13 ✸ T FOOKS

County Bridge, Charmouth, the subject of this delightful postcard view by Stengel & Co of London. It disappeared as part of road straightening and levelling in 1954.

measure indicative of contemporary attitudes to public property. Twenty or so still survive in situ and are worth seeking out. Some bridges were built by turnpike trusts, the Vale of Blackmoor funding the Coalbrookdale Iron Company to produce the iron bridge over the Lydden at Bagber, about 1830.

Although landowners were to be found supporting turnpike development, Dorset also has some good examples of landowner influence altering or frustrating the plans of turnpike trustees. The new Durweston bridge of 1795 allowed the old road to be diverted away from the Bryanston estate, and a plaque records its funding by the Portman family. Further north the present A350 takes a detour around three sides of Stepleton House at Iwerne Stepleton, instead of following the no doubt older and straighter route through the park, still a footpath today. In part, this detour is actually pre-turnpike. Other diversion stories can be traced at Frampton.

ROADS AND ROAD USERS

Road users and their vehicles varied enormously in their requirements of the network. Many people walked and others used horseback as their primary means of travel. A range of horse-drawn vehicles in private ownership might be seen on Dorset roads, including two-wheeled traps and carts and the more sophisticated carriages of the aristocracy and gentry. Indeed the nature of the conveyance was also a strong indicator of wealth and status, a point not missed on Dorset society.

Public services included the long-distance stage coaches and freight waggons plus the more local services of the town and village carriers. Tradesmen relied upon all these for receipt and despatch of their goods, as the letterbooks of Simon Pretor, a grocer and haberdasher and later a banker in Sherborne reveals. His business served customers for miles around at the end of the eighteenth century and he bought his goods and foodstuffs in London and Bristol, to be delivered either by waggon from Holborn or by the quicker service

In the phaeton on the downland at Langton Lodge in the winter of 1823; an example of early off-road activity?

offered on the Royal Clarence coach. Goods from Bristol and Exeter also came by road, using local services, and Pretor collected wine from Weymouth in his own waggon.

The picture is of a busy and regular network with substantial quantities of Dorset goods carried to London, such as sailcloth, woollen cloth, thrown silk, buttons, butter, wool and leather. Sherborne was well served by both coach and waggon services being on one of the major London routes. Woolcotts of Sherborne was a long established firm, based at the New Inn, and had workshops, stables and granaries around a courtyard.

From 1816 one of its main rivals was Thomas Russell & Co which became one of the largest carriers serving the West Country, operating services from The Bell in Cheapside through Dorset via Shaftesbury and via Dorchester and onwards to Exeter, Plymouth and Falmouth. In the early nineteenth century this company had up to 30 waggons and 200 horses in use, carrying an enormous variety of goods.

Thomas Russell & Co were one of the largest carriers serving the West Country, operating from The Bell in Cheapside through Dorset via Shaftesbury and Dorchester and onwards to Exeter, and Falmouth.

The White Horse Inn at Maiden Newton prior to its
rebuilding in the late 1890s.

There is a nice touch of rivalry between the two when Woolcott
started to compete on the route to Blandford in the following year.
One of the Russell partners took the view that Woolcott was better as
a rival on the road than forced off, such was his unreliability; 'could
we wish for a man who has less to recommend him: obstinate,
irregular, of dubious credit, constantly offending his customers'. It
was not always an easy journey. However, Woolcotts survived and
introduced a 'flying waggon' service to London in 1825, changing
teams and waggoners at intervals and so travelling continuously
rather than stopping over at night to rest the same team and crew.

A study of stage coach routes at the height of their influence
nationally in 1836 lists five coaches servicing the Exeter route on a
daily basis, most of them using what is now the A303 route north of
the county via Wincanton and Ilchester. The Magnet left the Belle
Sauvage Inn on Ludgate Hill (a major starting point for London's
coaches) each day at 5am on its 130-mile and 15-hour journey to
Weymouth, via Salisbury, Blandford and Dorchester. Two operators
in each case operated a daily one-way service between Bristol and
Weymouth and Bath and Weymouth, and J.Cockram & Co operated

A fine contrast in indolence and activity outside the Kings Arms in Dorchester, one of the town's two premier coaching inns (the other was the Antelope) and both rebuilt in the early nineteenth century.

a daily return journey between Exeter and Southampton.

By 1839 the system was probably working at its most extensive. Dorchester enjoyed no less than 16 coach visits each weekday, the most significant of which was the Royal Mail, also the fastest with a journey time from London of thirteen and a half hours. Part of a postal coaching network established in 1784 and replacing the humble post boy, two routes passed through the county, that between London and Devonport via Shaftesbury and that to Exeter via Dorchester.

In Dorchester the Antelope was one of the town's two main coaching inns, advertising itself in 1833 as a 'Commercial Inn and Posting House'. Another interesting piece of evidence as to how the system was measured from London survives on the Shire Hall of 1797 in High West Street, Dorchester, an inscription reading HYDE PARK CORNER 120/ BLANDFORD 16/ BRIDPORT 15. Elsewhere in the county, a milestone outside the Crown Inn in Blandford Forum also records the distance to Hyde Park Corner, at 104 miles, as well as to five other towns; another at Ferndown records '99 Miles to Hyde Park Corner through Ringwood'.

HYDE PARK CORNER 120
BLANDFORD 16
BRIDPORT 15

Distance marker on the Shire Hall in the centre of Dorchester.

The smaller carriers were also known as tranters, an altogether more humble affair than the long-distance carriers. Essentially they linked the villages with their nearest town, carrying people as well as goods, using a light cart or van and providing a regular and well-known service, coming in from the villages in the morning and returning at the end of the day. These carriers' networks developed in the eighteenth century and survived longer than more heavyweight

The daily horse bus service between Crewkerne station, Beaminster and Bridport, seen here about to leave the White Hart Commercial Hotel in Beaminster.

Mr Pitcher, the Litton Cheney carrier, successfully made the switch from the horse-drawn waggon to the motorised omnibus in the 1920s.

competitors, being able to adapt to the arrival of the railways by serving the local railway station (itself sometimes rather isolated) as an alternative and often additional destination.

Well into the twentieth century carriers still provided a comprehensive network, remaining a regular sight on the county's roads. Most came into Dorchester on Wednesdays and Saturdays, a recognition of market days, from as far away as Hazlebury Bryan in the north, Rampisham and Kingcombe to the west and Bere Regis to the east, some 42 all told in 1880.

This network became the nucleus of the later horse-drawn omnibus services which then formed a significant stage in the progression to motor transport on Dorset's roads. Frank Thorne, once a Cerne Abbas carrier, was driving a 32hp Albion bus on its daily journey into Dorchester by 1919, still with the word 'carrier' emblazoned on its side. In 1938 there were still 28 carriers serving the county town.

Although reaching Dorset comparatively later than elsewhere, it was the development of the railways which first challenged and then

This photograph may be of poor quality, but it is historic, and is one of
Dorset's earliest photographs, probably dating from the mid 1850s – a time
when the expanding railway network was making mail coaches redundant.
It shows the last London/Dorchester/Exeter mail coach outside the Coach
and Horses, Charmouth. The driver was called 'Tiny', the post boy
Sam Biles, and the man in the white waistcoat was Fred Wild,
who met all the mail coaches.

saw off the turnpike system and the coaching and carrying networks
on the roads. The line from Southampton to Dorchester opened in
1847, followed ten years later by the route into Weymouth from
Yeovil and beyond. Both mirrored the earlier turnpike routes and so
competed directly for business. Later railway routes did the same, the
line from Yeovil to Dorchester with its branch to Bridport from
Maiden Newton opening in 1857, and the line across the north of the
county between Shaftesbury and Sherborne (reached in 1860). The
Blackmore Vale gained immediate benefits from being opened up to
rail services from stations such as Gillingham.

There was a dramatic effect upon local coaching services by road.
In the same issue of the local newspaper announcing the 1857 railway
opening was an auction advertisement for '22 well-seasoned,
powerful, fast and well-bred coach horses' and 'three well-built

coaches' from the service between Yeovil and Weymouth.

The old ways were passing and little remains as evidence on the ground, other than some abandoned sections of old coach road, worth seeking out. Some old inns are also reminders, despite extensive modernisation. In the towns which the railways had missed, the effect was also marked and Beaminster and Cerne Abbas are good examples. The last stage coach ran through Cerne Abbas in 1855, leaving the small town isolated from such links with the outside world. Beaminster's population declined from 2,832 in 1851 to 1,702 fifty years later.

The roads and lanes of Dorset accommodated all sorts of vehicles, not always keeping out of each other's way. Hardy's *The Woodlanders* describes a meeting on the road in the fog between the sixteen-horse team, hauling the laden timber carriage from Melbury and complete with their sets of warning bells, and Mrs Charamond's brougham and carriage, whose coachman assumed a right of way. The argument which ensued says as much about status in rural Dorset society as about the practicalities of navigating in inclement weather or in the dark.

County fairs and markets would also fill up the roads with travellers and had done so since medieval times. Poundbury Sheep Fair was held on the last Thursday each September, drawing both people and animals along the byways and drongs (narrow ways) into Dorchester. An eyewitness recalled that 'the roads were white with dust from the droves of cattle and sheep'. Other fairs included Maiden Newton Fancy Fair as well as Woodbury Fair. To this should be added village celebrations of many kinds, at Easter, May Day and especially later that month at Whitsun, with club days, 'Club Walking' processions and folk returning to their villages for the annual get-together.

Bicycles became a very popular means of transport, the height of fashion for both men and women which caused a resurgence in road usage at the end of the nineteenth century. Cycling clubs became popular. Thomas Hardy became a keen cyclist in his fifties, undertaking many day trips of forty to fifty miles around the county and continuing well into his eighties.

HIGHWAYS AND MODERN ROADS

Despite the considerable improvements effected under the turnpike system, the fact remains that only about one-sixth of English roads were ever turnpiked, the remainder continuing as the responsibility of parish or town with all the well-known deficiencies in maintenance. Not until the General Highway Act of 1835 did this order of things much change. The parish was then enabled to levy a rate and so appoint a salaried surveyor, a first step towards the funding system for road management which evolved substantially through the remainder of the nineteenth century as the modern system of local government itself developed.

Key changes were made in 1848 when urban roads came under Local Boards of Health, and 1862 when parish roads were combined into Highway Districts under Highway Boards. The emergence of

The Old Charmouth Road, seen here heading towards the Devil's Bellows, the cutting down into Charmouth. The road was closed to traffic in 1924, and much of it has since collapsed into the sea.

A brewers' dray and cart from the Ansty Brewery outside the New Ox Inn at Shillingstone before 1900, on the Blandford to Sherborne road.

Urban and Rural District Councils under the 1894 Act brought most minor roads into the network, and a follow-up Act in 1929 brought the maintenance of rural roads into the care of the county councils.

Meanwhile the network of main roads had already come under county councils' care from their inception in 1888, with each establishing their own highway districts. This included responsibility

Angel Lane in Shaftesbury a century or so ago, its rough road surface free of the traffic which now clogs all of Dorset's towns and many of its villages. In this lane once stood the Angel, a coaching inn at 'the place where five roads meet' and since 1946 the site of the town's post office.

North Street in Wareham in a more gentle motoring age than now. On the left a garage complete with petrol pump and tyres stacked outside. In the background on North Walls is St. Martins Church.

for the maintenance of the former turnpike system (the last three Dorset trusts having expired on November 1 1882) with the power to add other significant roads; hence the phrase 'county road' cropping up on maps and in documents.

Improvements to the road surface have always presented a continuing challenge. Despite the efforts of turnpike trusts, conditions were often bad especially in winter; a correspondent in Dorset in 1812 found some minor roads still 'miry and scarcely passable in winter, and the large rough loose stones with which they abound render them very unpleasant in summer'.

It was the McAdam family, and especially John Loudon McAdam (1756-1836), who made the greatest improvements to road surfaces, not least in the West Country where he was Surveyor for the large Bristol Turnpike Trust from 1816-25. McAdam's name has entered the language meaning a smooth well-draining road surface, made up of small stones broken down to no more than an inch in dimension, which were laid without foundation directly upon the subsoil. The wear of passing traffic would then firmly bind them together. McAdam resisted any use of sand or earth as a binding agent. In Dorset the family's influence as surveyors for turnpike trusts included his son William at Cerne Abbas and Sturminster in the mid 1820s.

Various writers have left impressions of the bright white surface of

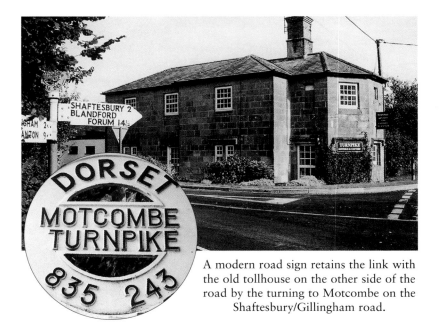

A modern road sign retains the link with the old tollhouse on the other side of the road by the turning to Motcombe on the Shaftesbury/Gillingham road.

the road, reflected in the sunshine. Revd Francis Kilvert described his visit to Revd William Barnes on 'May Eve' in 1874, when he walked out from Fordington in Dorchester to the rectory at Winterbourne Came, which lay 'a little back from the glaring white high road'. Later the writer H.S. Joyce described the country roads of his childhood in the later nineteenth century around Sturminster Marshall, the surface made up of broken flints, piles of which were dumped at the roadside to be broken up and then laid. Initially this was done by hand until the arrival of the noisy and impressive council steam roller, which really came into its own with the introduction of tarmacadam as the preferred modern road surface during the 1920s.

McAdam's philosophy had been to improve the road surface to take account of users' requirements, rather than use tolls and charges to discourage certain types of road use such as heavy waggons. In this he paved the way for subsequent road improvements. This also foreshadowed the emergence of the automobile. By 1906 there were over 45,000 licensed motor vehicles, and nearly 389,000 by the outbreak of the First World War in 1914. Of these 1,200 were in

A County Council road gang outside Sturminster Newton in the early 1930s, when the horse was still used to pull the water wagon.

Dorset, observing a universal speed limit of 20mph. In 1907 Lyme Regis Borough Council had decided that 'motor car signs' were needed to deal with these new traffic concerns.

Other road signs had started to appear, both from local authorities and the emerging motorists associations, the Royal Automobile Club (RAC) and the Automobile Association (AA), the latter installing in the 1920s its own circular yellow and black place name signs at the entrance to towns and villages. Some of the earliest road signs were actually for cyclists in the 1880s. Standardisation of road signs dates from 1933 and again in 1963 when the present-day system emerges, compatible with the European pictorial system.

Like many counties Dorset still has examples from all these periods, scarce though they are becoming. Thankfully, in response to such standardisation, the concept of 'local distinctiveness' continues to gain ground, where examples of earlier and perhaps more locally-created types are adopted (often at parish council level) as valuable historic treasures with their own character.

Seen now in hindsight, the government announcements in 1940 that road signs and signposts, and shortly afterwards milestones and mileposts too, were to be removed lest they provide guidance for an

One of Dorset's unique finger posts, dating to between 1948 and 1964, and in which both the place name and grid reference are given.

invading enemy seems far-fetched, but they were serious issues at the time. Many examples were removed as a result, often recycled into the wartime scrap effort, never to be seen again. Others re-appeared after the war from council depots and sometimes were re-excavated from their place of burial.

Dorset has its own distinctive finger posts which are topped off by circular finials in aluminium proclaiming both place name and grid reference. Although dating only from 1948-64, and the inspiration of the then county surveyor, J.J. Leeming, they are very much part of the county's road heritage. In 1930 the Ministry of Transport had asked Dorset and West Riding county councils to experiment with grid references on their signs, and these are the result. Today with growing public interest a repair and renewals programme is under way.

Mystery surrounds why three finger posts are painted red rather than the usual white, near Benville Bridge, to the north of Sherborne, and at Winterborne Tomson. Each is marked on OS maps as Red Post. Another can be found at Hewood, four miles southeast of Chard. Various interpretations include the sites of gibbets, of suicides, as markers on convict transportation routes, or as parish boundary meeting places. Were there once others and did they perhaps mark significant junctions on old cross-country routes?

The modern road network is a product of an immensely long history, with further dramatic changes in the last half-century, drawing

One of Dorset's small number of Red Posts; why they are painted this colour remains a mystery.

down central government funds and affecting at least the major roads into and through the county. By-passes to towns and villages are a key feature of this, gradually getting longer and making greater impact on the landscape than ever before, as at Blandford, Dorchester, Wareham and all around Poole. There are also long sections of rural 'by-passing' such as the nearly six miles of A35 around Tolpuddle and Puddletown, opened in 1999 with its £25m cost funded in an innovative way using private as well as public finance. The knock-on effects of traffic dispersal around the whole road network, including Dorset's hundreds of miles of country lanes, remains a continuing issue for local debate.

In many ways the wheel has run full circle, in that nationally tolls are returning into use for specific road developments where great expense is involved, and various forms of direct taxation of the motorist as the primary user reflect the basic concept of the turnpike trusts of the eighteenth and nineteenth centuries. The road network belongs to all those who use it, and in some form or another everybody contributes to the cost of its upkeep and future development. Especially in a largely rural county such as Dorset, it remains recognisably based upon historical development, the evidence of which remains all around for exploration and enjoyment.

SEARCHING THE OLD ROUTES

Opportunities to examine the old ways on foot, by bicycle or car are legion in Dorset, and much information is available from Dorset County Council's excellent range of information points and literature to provide access and other details. Here it has only been possible to suggest a limited number of routes, usually with a strong period theme, to illustrate what can be enjoyed in the landscape. Good companions are Jo Draper's *Dorset: The Complete Guide* and her *Walking Dorset History* with Christopher Chaplin.

Much of the Dorset Ridgeway long-distance route can be followed over 60 miles across Dorset from Shaftesbury to beyond Lyme Regis and good sections of this route can be walked. Smugglers Lane leads down to the crossing of the Stour between Hod and Hambledon Hills,

At Folly, the Dorset Ridgeway is crossed by the road between Plush and Mappowder, the track following the tree line up the hill towards Ball Hill. This is a splendid walk, now part of the Wessex Ridgeway, and runs right across north Dorset. The building was once the Folly Inn, remote on its hilltop and closed over sixty years ago.

A Vale of Blackmoor Trust toll board showing the wide range of rates charged in 1824 at the Horsington turnpike gate north of Templecombe.

both significant prehistoric sites. Westwards is a high level route by path and track over Bell Hill, Bulbarrow (where some eight routes meet) and the Dorsetshire Gap en route towards Cerne Abbas.

A drive from Dogbury Gate (ST 656053) north of Cerne on A352 westwards over Batcombe via Holywell, Evershot and Benville Bridge to join the A356 at Toller Down Gate probably follows the line of the Ridgeway route, later turnpiked.

Further west, there is a good walk along the track from Beaminster

In this 1938 view the Roman road from Dorchester to Ilchester descends as a track to pass under Grimstone viaduct between Stratton and Frampton

Down over Horn Hill and along Common Water Lane to Broadwindsor. An alternative Ridgeway route cuts across the north side of Lewesdon Hill by the lane westwards from Stoke Knapp (ST 445015-425017). This track, a delightful walk amongst the beech trees, has a long history, and may even be a Roman route. It certainly is part of a medieval and post medieval route around Marshwood Vale.

Much of the South Dorset Ridgeway can be enjoyed as part of the South West Coast Path, and also between Corfe Castle and Swanage on the Purbeck Way, providing a memorable walk of some 30 miles.

In and around Cranborne Chase are two fine early routes. From A354, the Ox Drove can be followed westwards across spectacular country to Win Green (ST 925206) and on across Ashmore Down. The Salisbury Way, although in neighbouring Wiltshire, should be included here as a fine 13-mile high-level downland walk from Salisbury to Whitesheet Hill, to drop down to A30 and the old turnpike road some two miles east of Shaftesbury (ST 933240).

The best of the Roman routes is Ackling Dyke, accessible from B3081 at SU 016164 off Handley roundabout on A354. From here the route can be followed on foot for over nine miles towards Badbury Rings, where the ancient monument (ST 963030) can also be visited as a National Trust site.

Other shorter sections can be followed on foot or by car. The old and direct line of the Dorchester to Weymouth road over Ridgeway Hill is now a section of two long-distance footpaths; the modern road

White Post toll house on the Wincanton road from Sherborne

takes a more easterly zig-zag route. A short section of the Roman road to Ilchester is now a footpath west of Stratton to Grimstone viaduct.

The Eggardon road from Dorchester is a delightful drive, and the regional capital itself is always worth exploring, the footprint of the Roman town still apparent within the walled and defended area. All the major roads into and out of Dorchester continue to reflect historic alignments from Roman times onwards.

Central Dorset has plenty of ridgeway and cross-ridge routes, some labelled as drove ways. Furzy Down Road (still called this in 1765) runs north from Grimstone west of Stratton on A37 (SY 642938) and offers a fine walk to Gore Hill, linking with several medieval and monastic routes. The old road between Dorchester and Shaftesbury going over Bulbarrow strikes off from the Piddle valley near Waterston Corner (SY 728958) making for Dole's Hill Plantation, where a network of routes can be traced on old maps. Some drove routes can also be walked, such as Stonerush Drove west of Hermitage.

On Purbeck, the Priests Way is waymarked by modern stone markers, providing an invigorating walk, with access via Durnford Drove and Spyway Barn (SY 999778).

Careful map study will reveal sections of road abandoned either as a consequence of the first introduction of turnpikes or just as frequently as the result of subsequent improvements. Gainsborough Hill and Green Lane coming south from Sherborne is one good example, where the turnpike was later moved to its present alignment further west. Another is the old way up the bank at Winyard's Gap,

[73]

now a lane and holloway to the north of its replacement by the Maiden Newton Trust (ST 492063). Before 1820 the road from Morcombelake to Charmouth went up Ship Knapp and over Stonebarrow Hill, an accessible route today (car park at SY 383934).

In all the principal towns it is still possible to identify some of the former coaching inns, albeit much altered. Recent surveys suggest there are at least thirty surviving toll houses in Dorset, many also considerably modernised. This is perhaps no more than one third of the original total. A greater appreciation of their historic significance should aid preservation, compared to the loss of no less than nine examples between 1963-77 at a time of considerable road improvement. Good examples are in Bridport, Charmouth, Charminster and Sherborne. Milestones can be found on all the major routes, their variety another form of local distinctiveness.

Charborough Park's boundary wall to the A31 includes Lion Gate and Stag Gate, contemporary with the turnpike scheme and a physical reminder of aristocratic influence. Two milestones are incorporated within it. Horn Hill tunnel remains in use, although Charmouth tunnel is now on private land. The most obvious example of twentieth century change of access are the restrictions associated with military use around the Lulworth ranges, especially the old routes down to Tyneham and the coast.

Old routes and green lanes are becoming more popular, promoted as key features in increasing access to the countryside. They are finding a new role for leisure use to replace their earlier functional role as historic links between communities. The National Cycle Network makes use of old as well as new routes across Dorset.

The displays in Dorset County Museum include the fragment of Roman milestone from Dorchester and an example of the Fooks transportation warning sign removed in 1927 from South Bridge at Wareham. Gillingham Museum has two AA roundel signs plus the toll boards from the Purns Mill and Madjeston gates, whilst Salisbury Museum has the one from New Cross Gate on the Blandford to Sturminster Newton road, all on the Vale of Blackmoor Turnpike. Ringwood Meeting House Museum has the '92 Miles to Hyde Park Corner' wall plate from a local toll house.

Finally, even when no structures survive, place name evidence is not

The top photograph shows Athelhampton toll-house a few years after its sale in 1878 when it was a lodge of Athelhampton House. The lower photograph records its re-opening in 1999, following its restoration: it is now accessible to visitors to the house.

hard to find whilst driving in Dorset. Birdsmoor Gate (ST 392009) is still recognisably a junction of routes and so is New Cross Gate (ST 812124). However Revels Inn (ST 676055) is no more, nor Long Bredy Hut, now a fast section on A35 where a lane climbs out of the Bride valley to the south (SY 569913). An inn was built here in 1753 alongside the tollgate, a recognised if isolated refreshment stop for coach traffic.

FURTHER READING

Albert, William, *The Turnpike Road System in England 1663-1840*, Cambridge 1972

Beaton, David, *Dorset Maps*, Dovecote Press 2001

Chubb, Linda et al, *Dorset Toll-House Survey*, Dorset County Council Countryside Treasures series, 1977

Cochrane, C, *The Lost Roads of Wessex*, David & Charles, 1969

Cox, R. Hippisley, *The Green Roads of England*, Methuen 1914

Eedle, Marie de G, *Horn Hill Tunnel*, published by the author, 1994

Gerhold, Dorian, *Road Transport before the Railways: Russell's London Flying Waggons*, Cambridge 1993. See also 'A Dorset Carrier in 1830' in *PDNHAS*, vol.115 for 1993, pp.29-32 (Woolcotts)

Good, Ronald, *The Old Roads of Dorset*, 1st edition, Dorset Nat. History & Archaeological Society, 1940 and 2nd enlarged edition, Commin, Bournemouth 1966

Gow, W.G., *Dorset Milestone Survey*, Dorset County Council Countryside Treasures series, 1980

James, Jude, *Dorset Turnpike Roads*, Dorset Archaeological Committee, revised 2000. See also 'The Road to Ruin: The Wimborne to Puddletown Turnpike, 1841', in *The Hatcher Review*, vol. 4, no 39 Spring 1995, pp.35-43.

Le Fleming, E. Kaye, 'The Records of the Turnpike Trustees of the Wimborne and Cranborne Trust', *Dorset Procs*, vol. 48 for 1927, pp.59-69

Miller, A.J., *Poole Turnpike Trust 1756-1882*, Poole 1977

Stanier, Peter, *Dorset's Industrial Heritage*, Twelveheads Press, 1989; *The Industrial Past* in the Discover Dorset series, Dovecote Press, 1998; and *Dorset in the Age of Steam: a History and Archaeology of Dorset Industry c.1750-1950*, Dorset Books, Halsgrove, 2002

Taylor, C., *Dorset*, Hodder & Stoughton 1970 and *Roads and Tracks of Britain*, Dent 1979

Timperley, H.W. and Brill, Edith, *Ancient Trackways of Wessex*, Phoenix House 1965; new edition Nonsuch Publishing 2005

Viner, David, 'The Wimborne and Puddletown Turnpike Trust (1841-78) and the Toll-house at Athelhampton' in *PDNHAS*, vol.104 for 1982, pp.25-32

Weinstock, M.B., 'Beaminster-Bridport Turnpike' in *More Dorset Studies*, Dorchester 1960, pp.69-73

Wright, G.N., *Roads and Trackways of Wessex*, Moorland Publishing 1988

ACKNOWLEDGEMENTS

Many Dorset local historians have assisted my research over the years, too many to acknowledge individually, but especial thanks are due to Peter Stanier, John Lowe, Historic Buildings Officer for Dorset County Council, and to John Tybjerg and other members of the Milestone Society who have shared my enthusiasms. Amongst other Dorset friends, very little would have been achieved without the encouragement over many years from Jo Draper and Christopher Chaplin, who generously gave freely of their extensive Dorset knowledge, copying many references and providing a base in the county for fieldwork and research, about as close as one can get to the Dorset Record Office, which also now includes the Dorset History Centre. Thanks are due to the staff both here and in the Dorset County Museum for their stewardship and advice. Jo Draper and John Tybjerg kindly commented on and improved a draft of the text. Last but not least, to coin a familiar author's phrase, none of this would have been possible without the patient support of my wife, Linda, whose fondness for the county of Dorset fully mirrors my own.

I would like to thank the following for allowing the use of illustrations in their possession or for which they hold the copyright:

Patrick Cooke (AthelhamptonHall), page 75 (bottom): Dorset County Museum, pages 35, 39, 44 (left), 57, 59 (bottom), 60, 61: Dorset Records Office, pages 34 [D606/3/1 (31)], 72 [D606/3/1 (6)], The Fitzwilliam Museum, Cambridge, back cover and page 9: Lyme Regis Museum: page 40: the watercolour by Diana Sperling taken from *Mrs Hurst Dancing & Other Scenes from Regency Life 1812-1823* (Gollanz 1981), page 55: Peter Stanier, page 13: University of Cambridge, Department of Aerial Photographs, frontispiece, page 19. The remaining illustrations are from the author's collection or that of The Dovecote Press.

I am grateful to Nick Griffiths for drawing the maps on pages 6 and 27.

The Milestone Society, formed in 2000, campaigns for the recording and conservation of roadside heritage including milestones and waymarkers. See www.milestone-society.co.uk

INDEX

The

DISCOVER DORSET

Series of Books

A series of paperback books providing informative illustrated
introductions to Dorset's history, culture and way of life.
The following titles have so far been published.

BLACKMORE VALE *Hilary Townsend*

BRIDGES *David McFetrich and Jo Parsons*

CASTLES AND FORTS *Colin Pomeroy*   COAST & SEA *Sarah Welton*

CRANBORNE CHASE *Desmond Hawkins*

DOWNS, MEADOWS & PASTURES *Jim White*

DRESS AND TEXTILES *Rachel Worth*

FARMHOUSES & COTTAGES *Michael Billett*

FARMING *J.H. Bettey*   FOLLIES *Jonathan Holt*

FOSSILS *Richard Edmonds*   GEOLOGY *Paul Ensom*

THE GEORGIANS *Jo Draper*   HEATHLANDS *Lesley Haskins*

THE INDUSTRIAL PAST *Peter Stanier*

ISLE OF PURBECK *Paul Hyland*   LEGENDS *Jeremy Harte*

LOST VILLAGES *Linda Viner*   MILLS *Peter Stanier*

PORTLAND *Stuart Morris*   POTTERY *Penny Copland-Griffiths*

THE PREHISTORIC AGE *Bill Putnam*   RAILWAY STATIONS *Mike Oakley*

REGENCY, RIOT & REFORM *Jo Draper*

RIVERS & STREAMS *John Wright*

ROADS, TRACKS & TURNPIKES *David Viner*

THE ROMANS *Bill Putnam*   SAXONS & VIKINGS *David Hinton*

SHIPWRECKS *Maureen Attwooll*   STONE QUARRYING *Jo Thomas*

TUDORS & STUARTS *J.H. Bettey*

THE VICTORIANS *Jude James*   WOODLANDS *Anne Horsfall*

All the books about Dorset published by The Dovecote Press
are available in bookshops throughout the county,
or in case of difficulty direct from the publishers.
The Dovecote Press Ltd, Stanbridge, Wimborne Minster, Dorset BH21 4JD
Tel: 01258 840549 www.dovecotepress.com